FUTURES TRADING STRATEGIES

*Enter and Exit the Market Like a Pro with Proven
and Powerful Techniques For Profits*

WAYNE WALKER

Table of Contents

INTRODUCTION

Congratulations on your personal copy of *Futures Trading Strategies*. This book will ensure that you are equipped to begin using futures contracts as a trading instrument. We will examine proven futures trade entry techniques along with the technical analysis strategy needed to execute them.

The book is primarily about futures trading, however the futures market can be, and often is, influenced by other markets. In the later chapters we will look at these markets individually and in the last chapter you will be introduced to exchange traded funds (ETFs), one of the most important and useful products created for individual investors in recent years.

There are plenty of books on the market, thanks for choosing this one.

CHAPTER 1

FUTURES OVERVIEW

You have probably heard from friends or in the media of traders profiting from the futures market and you may have asked yourself if you could also profit from these global price fluctuations. The answer: yes, you too can participate in the futures market with a trading account.

The futures market is exciting and broad because it allows you to trade futures contracts on everything from cotton and sugar to interest rates and energies. You are not limited to just one sector of the global economy nor to strong economic periods. As a trader you can make money when prices are going up and also when prices are going down in the futures market.

Futures Contracts

The base of the futures market is the futures contract. To participate in the futures market you need to understand what a futures contract is and how it works. Let us begin with a basic definition and then we will move to a more in-depth understanding of the contracts and how you can profit from them. A futures contract is a contract between a buyer and a seller wherein the seller agrees to deliver a commodity/underlying instrument to the buyer on a specified date for a specified price.

Contracts

Buyers and sellers create futures contracts. This may seem odd at first if you are familiar with trading stocks which are issued by companies that determine the number of shares available. Futures contracts are different from stock market shares. While there is a finite number of stock market shares available, in contrast, there is an infinite number of potential futures contracts available. As long as there is a buyer and a seller, together they can create a futures contract.

Futures exchanges track how many contracts are created and list the amount as volume. Volume tells you how many contracts are created for each available commodity during each trading period. For example if you were looking at the natural gas futures contract and you saw a volume of 75,000 then you would know that 75,000 contracts had been created that day for the natural gas futures.

Volume can reveal a lot about what is going on with a futures contract and how many people are trading it, but it doesn't provide you the whole picture because not all volume comes from traders opening new trades. A sizable amount of volume is generated by traders who are already in trades and want to exit their trades.

4

Futures traders who are in a trade and want to get out of a trade have to create a new contract to offset their other contract.

As a futures trader you need to be aware of not only how many contracts have been created but also how many of those contracts remain active. High volume and high open interest are signs of good liquidity in the market, which means it should be very easy for you to quickly enter and exit your own trades at a small spread between the bid and ask price. Low volume and low open interest are signs of poor liquidity in the market, which means it will be most likely difficult for you to quickly enter and exit your trades at a good price.

Bid and Ask Price

Let us take a look at the buyers and sellers of the contracts. Futures contracts are quoted in two prices: a bid price and an ask price. The bid price is the price you receive when you sell your futures contracts. The ask price is the price offered when you want to buy futures contracts. The bid price is always lower than the ask price, and the difference between the two is called the spread. When a contract has low volume, the spread between the bid and the ask will be wide. When a futures contract has high volume, the spread between the bid and the ask will be thin or small. As a futures trader, or a trader in general, you want the spread to be as small as possible.

You can be either a buyer or a seller of a futures contract. The futures market provides great flexibility to buy or sell. As long as there is someone on the other side willing to sell a contract you want to buy, or to buy a contract you want to sell, you can create the contract.

Long and Short Positions

Two terms that you will hear often when discussing buying and selling futures contracts are long and short. To go long on a contract means to buy the contract. To go short on a contract means to sell the contract.

Typically, futures traders look to buy a contract when they believe the price is going to go up, and they want to sell a contract when they believe the price is going to go down. Your job as a futures trader is to determine in which direction you believe the price is going to move and trade accordingly.

Futures contract prices fluctuate daily and some futures exchanges limit the distance some contracts can move in one trading period. Futures contracts with maximum price fluctuation rules attached to them will stop trading if they move too far in one direction.

Futures contracts also have what are known as limit up and limit down thresholds. If the price of the futures contract moves up too high or down too low, trading on that contract will stop for a few minutes to allow the exchange to determine if trading should continue that day or if it should be halted to prevent panic on the exchange floor.

Hedgers and Speculators

Buyers and sellers of futures contracts are usually divided into two groups: hedgers and speculators.

Hedgers are traders who use futures contracts to hedge risks they face by dealing with the actual underlying commodities (ex. a wheat farmer) and the price swings associated with them.

Speculators are traders who use futures contracts to speculate on and hopefully profit from price changes in the underlying commodities. Speculators typically do NOT deal with the underlying commodities covered by the futures contract in their day-to-day business. You will most likely fall into this category of futures traders.

Speculators buy futures contracts on commodities that they believe are going to increase in value and sell futures contracts on commodities that they believe are going to fall in value. Speculators play an important role in the futures market. They provide liquidity for hedgers who are looking to offset their risk. Speculators take on risk when they enter a trade. In plain terms, hedgers pass their risks on to speculators who hope to profit from them.

Now that you have a basic understanding of who the buyers and sellers in the futures market are, let us take a look at the commodities those buyers and sellers are trading.

CHAPTER 2

COMMODITY FUTURES

Commodity Futures

When many people think of the commodity futures market they think about trading coffee or orange juice. While these commodities trade on the futures exchanges, they make up a smaller portion of the trading activity. Nowadays oil contracts, natural gas contracts, interest-rate contracts, grains and others dominate the futures market.

The futures market offers a broad and diverse array of contracts which you can trade. You can profit from falling oil prices and you can take advantage of a raising currency. You can divide the available futures contracts into two categories: commodity futures and financial futures.

Commodity futures are futures contracts that are based on a physical commodity that you can raise, grow, mine and transport from place to place. Commodity futures comprise the following sectors:

- Agriculture

- Base Metals

- Energies

- Meats

- Precious Metals

- Softs

Financial futures are futures contracts that are based on financial products like bonds and stock indices. Financial futures comprise the following futures sectors:

- Bonds

- Currencies

- Short-term Interest Rates

- Stock Indices

Within each of these sectors you will find contracts ranging from sugar and soya beans to silver and copper, and each contract has a unique personality. We will cover several of these sectors and the contracts within them in later chapters.

CHAPTER 3

CONTRACTS DATES, EXCHANGES AND MARGINS

Contracts Dates

Every futures contract has a specified date on which it expires and a specified price at which the seller must provide the commodity and the buyer must pay for it. We will take a look at the dates involved with a contract, and then we will take a look at the actual delivery of the underlying commodity.

Futures contracts have three key dates of which you need to be familiar with: Notice date, Expiry date, Delivery date.

The **Notice date** is the first day the seller of a futures contract can give the buyer of the contract notice to expect delivery of the underlying commodity. For example, if you sell a crude copper futures contract, you can give notice to the buyer of the contract that you will be delivering the actual copper. In reality you will not do this, you will instead offset your contracts before taking delivery.

The **Expiry date** is the day that the futures contract expires. It is also the last trading day for the contract. Futures contracts expire every month, however, not every commodity is traded each month, but there are always some commodity contracts available each month. You need to check the specific commodity you are trading to see when the contract expires.

Every futures contract has a unique ticker symbol that tells you what the underlying commodity is and when the contract expires. Each ticker symbol is broken up into three parts: the instrument identification, the month of expiration and the year of expiration. For example the ticker symbol for a Crude Oil contract that expires in July of 2017 is CLN17. CL represents the instrument, N represents the month of expiration, 17 represents the year of expiration.

The monthly commodity symbols are below:

F	January
G	February
H	March
J	April
K	May
M	June
N	July
Q	August
U	September

V	October
X	November
Z	December

The **Delivery date** is the last date by which the underlying commodity must be delivered from the seller to the buyer. The delivery date is also known as the settlement date. However, the seller does not have to wait until the delivery date to deliver the commodity. The seller can deliver at any time during the delivery period, the period between the first notice date and the delivery date.

Again, there is no need to worry about delivering or receiving delivery of a commodity you are trading. You should offset your positions before your contracts expire. In fact most traders, both speculators and hedgers, offset their positions. Only a small percentage of futures contracts actually go to delivery.

It is important to know that there are two types of delivery on futures contracts: physical delivery and cash-settled delivery. Physical delivery occurs when the buyer receives the underlying commodity from the contract. Cash-settled delivery occurs when, instead of trying to receive an intangible asset like the S&P 500, the buyer receives the cash equivalent of what the underlying asset would be worth.

You now have the basic information that you need to understand what a futures contract is. Let us take a look at where and how you actually trade a futures contract.

Futures Brokerages

A futures broker or a bank are your portal to the futures market. Your futures broker provides you with access to a trading platform and an account that allows you to buy and sell contracts. Your broker also provides you with the tools that you will need to research and monitor your trades.

Futures Exchanges

When you place a trade to buy or sell a contract your bank or broker sends that trade to a futures exchange for execution. In the past your trade would have been sent to the trading pit on the floor of the exchange for whatever contract you were trading. Floor traders would negotiate prices and your trade would be filled. Some trades are still executed on physical trading floors, many more are now executed online electronically. Complex software match buyers with sellers and execute trades in fractions of a second. Technological advances like these have made trading more efficient.

Here is a list of some of the exchanges on which you can trade:

Chicago Board of Trade (CBOT), via ECBOT

Chicago Mercantile Exchange (CME), via GLOBEX

New York Mercantile Exchange (NYMEX), via GLOBEX

New York Board of Trade (NYBOT), via ICE NYBOT

GLOBEX

Eurex

Euronext

ICE

Borsa Italiana

London International Financial Futures Exchange (LIFFE)

Spanish Official Exchange (MEFF)

OMX Stockholm (SSE)

Now that you know where you can trade futures contracts, let us take a look at how you actually go about placing your trades.

Margin Requirements

For many, one of the most tricky concepts to understand as a new futures trader is the concept of margin. When you trade a futures contract you do not pay for the full value of the underlying commodity up front as you would when trading stocks. Instead, you place a trade and deposit your margin with your futures broker verifying that you have sufficient money to cover any losses you may have from the trade.

For example, to buy a 1,000 barrels crude oil futures contract, instead of having to pay $50,000 for 1,000 barrels of crude oil (at a market rate of $50 per barrel) up front you would only need $3,500(for example purposes only) in your account as margin. This allows you to be able to withstand some losses on this trade should they come.

The margin you set aside when you enter a trade is called your initial margin. After executing a trade you may not need to maintain the same level of margin. When you are in a trade, you only need to meet what is called your maintenance margin requirement, which, depending on the exchange, is typically lower. Maintenance margin is the amount of money you must set aside to remain in a trade. In our crude oil example your maintenance margin requirement would only be $3,000, compared to the initial margin requirement of $3,500.

Margin requirements are set by the futures clearing houses. Margin requirements are also not permanently fixed. The exchange/clearing houses can adjust minimum margin requirements at any time. Your broker can raise their margin requirements if they want to. Your broker can also issue what is known as a margin call if your margin levels fall below acceptable minimums based on losses you have accumulated on your trades or increases in margin requirements. If you receive a margin call then you must deposit more money into your account to cover your margin obligations.

Once you have met your margin requirement, you can enter your trade. You can buy or sell a futures contract using either a market or a limit order. A market order is a buy or sell order that instructs your broker to place the trade at the current market rate. A limit order is a buy or sell order that instructs your broker to place the trade at a specific price or better.

If you want to enter or exit a trade quickly and ensure you get in or out then you should use a market order. If you are okay with waiting to enter or exit a trade until the price is just right then you could use a limit order to ensure you get the price you desire.

CHAPTER 4

COMMODITY SUPPLIERS

Futures contract prices rise and fall with the seasons of the year. The movements appear to flow in what seems to be a predictable rhythm, prices seem to always go up at certain times of the year and down at other times of the year. Whether it is spring planting season for agricultural commodities, a summer vacation low for equities, or December demand for precious metals, there always seems to be something on the calendar that influences supply and demand in the market.

This ebb and flow of prices is certainly not an exact science, many factors other than seasonality will have an influence on the price of a futures contract too, but knowing how the futures contracts you are watching progress through the seasonal calendar can help you plan your trading year and prepare for future trades.

To help give you a broad overview of your trading calendar and which futures contracts you may want to be buying or selling at any given time, we will discuss the characteristics of the four seasons of the year: Winter, Spring, Summer, Autumn.

Suppliers

Before we move into the seasons, it is important to know who the major suppliers of each commodity are so you can better understand why the change of seasons affects each one.

In today's global economy, the commodities we consume can come from virtually anywhere in the world. Often we hear about economic mega-centers like the United States, the European Union and China and we begin to think that everything we buy comes from these places. When you are dealing with raw commodities, however, that is not always true. Countries like Brazil, Argentina, India and even Peru are dominant producers of many of the commodities that trade on the global futures markets.

As you think about commodity producers, especially those that produce agricultural commodities it is important to remember which hemisphere they are in because that will have an influence on crop cycles. When it is summer in the Northern Hemisphere, it is winter in the Southern Hemisphere, and vice versa.

Northern Hemisphere: Is the half of earth that is north of the equator which is around 90% of the earth's total human population.

Southern Hemisphere: Is the half of earth that is south of the equator which is around 10% of the earth's total human population.

Let us review the top three producers for each of the following commodities: Energies, Precious Metals, Agriculture.

Energy

Crude Oil - The top three global producers of crude oil are as follows:

1. Russia

2. Saudi Arabia

3. United States

Natural Gas - The top three global producers of natural gas are as follows:

1. Russia

2. United States

3. Iran

Precious metals

Gold - The top three global producers of gold are as follows:

1. China

2. Australia

3. Russia

Silver - The top three global producers of silver are as follows:

1. Mexico

2. China

3. Peru

Agriculture

Soybeans - The top three global producers of soybeans are as follows:

1. United States

2. Brazil

3. Argentina

Wheat - The top three global producers of wheat are as follows:

1. China

2. India

3. Russia

Corn - The top three global producers of corn are as follows:

1. United States

2. China

3. Brazil

Sugar - The top three global producers of sugar are as follows:

1. Brazil

2. India

3. China

Coffee - The top three global producers of coffee are as follows:

1. Brazil

2. Vietnam

3. Colombia

Cotton - The top three global producers of cotton are as follows:

1. China

2. India

3. United States

CHAPTER 5

SEASONALITY AND THE FUTURES MARKET

Now that you know who the major producers of each commodity are, let us take a look at what you should be watching for in each season of the year.

January, February & March

Sugar

Winter in the Northern Hemisphere is harvest time for sugarcane and sugar beets. The sugarcane and sugar beet harvest has a noticeable impact on supply in the market. If it is a good harvest, supply will increase, which should decrease the price of sugar. If it is a poor or weak harvest, supply will decrease, which normally should increase the price of sugar.

April, May & June

Crude Oil

Crude oil prices typically begin to increase in the spring as gasoline producers begin to anticipate the well-known summer driving season in the United States.

Corn

Spring in the Northern Hemisphere is *planting* time for corn. The corn planting season has a direct impact on supply in the market. If it is a strong planting season, supply will increase, which should result in a decrease the price of corn. If it is a poor planting season, supply will decrease, which should increase the price of corn. Spring in the Southern Hemisphere is *harvest* time for corn. The corn harvest has a direct impact on supply in the market. If it is a good harvest, supply will increase, which should decrease the price of corn. If it is a poor harvest, supply will decrease, which should increase the price of corn.

Cotton

Spring in the Northern Hemisphere is planting time for cotton. The cotton planting season has a direct impact on supply in the market. If it is a strong planting season, supply will increase, which should decrease the price of cotton. If it is a poor planting season, supply will decrease, which should increase the price of cotton.

Soybeans

Spring in the Northern Hemisphere is *planting* time for soybeans. The soybean planting season has a direct impact on supply in the market. If it is a productive planting season, supply will increase, which should decrease the price of soybeans. If it is a poor planting season, supply will decrease, which should increase the price of soybeans. Spring in the Southern Hemisphere is *harvest* time for soybeans. The soybean harvest has a direct impact on supply in the market. If it is a good harvest, supply will increase, which should decrease the price of soybeans. If it is a poor harvest, supply will decrease, which should increase the price of soybeans.

Sugar

Spring in the Northern Hemisphere is *planting* time for sugarcane and sugar beets. The sugarcane and sugar beet planting season has a direct impact on supply in the market. If it is a productive planting season, supply will increase, which should decrease the price of sugar. If it is a poor planting season, supply will decrease, which should increase the price of sugar. Autumn in the Southern Hemisphere is *harvest* time for sugarcane and sugar beets. The sugarcane and sugar beet harvest has a direct impact on supply in the market. If it is a good harvest, supply will increase, which should decrease the price of sugar. If it is a poor harvest, supply will decrease, which should increase the price of sugar.

July, August & September

Crude Oil

Crude oil prices typically jump the most during the summer season as the amount of drivers on the road increase during the summer and producers of winter heating oil are increasing their supplies to sell at the start of the autumn.

Wheat

Summer in the Northern Hemisphere is traditional harvest time for wheat. The wheat harvest has a direct impact on supply in the market. If it is a good harvest, supply will increase, which should decrease the price of wheat. If it is a weak harvest, supply will decrease, which should normally increase the price of wheat.

Coffee

Winter in the Southern Hemisphere is harvest time for coffee. The coffee harvest has a clear impact on supply in the market. If it is a strong harvest, supply will increase, which should decrease the price of coffee. If it is a bad harvest, supply will decrease, which should increase the price of coffee.

Sugar

Winter in the Southern Hemisphere is also harvest time for sugarcane and sugar beets. The sugarcane and sugar beet harvest has a direct impact on supply in the market. If it is a strong harvest, supply will increase, which should decrease the price of sugar. If it is a poor harvest, supply will decrease, which should increase the price of sugar.

October, November & December

Crude Oil

Crude oil prices typically decrease the most during the autumn months as people begin to drive less. Also, people tend to buy most of their heating oil at the beginning of the season leaving less demand during the rest of the season.

Wheat

Autumn in the Northern Hemisphere is planting time for wheat. The wheat planting season has a direct impact on supply in the market. If it is a productive planting season, supply will increase, which should decrease the price of wheat. If it is a bad planting season, supply will decrease, which should increase the price of wheat.

Corn

Autumn in the Northern Hemisphere is harvest time for corn. The corn harvest has a direct impact on supply in the market. If it is a good harvest, supply will increase, which should decrease the price of corn. If it is a poor harvest, supply will decrease, which should increase the price of corn.

Cotton

Autumn in the Northern Hemisphere is harvest time for cotton. The cotton harvest has a direct impact on supply in the market. If it is a good harvest, supply will increase, which should decrease the price of cotton. If it is a weak harvest, supply will decrease, which should increase the price of cotton.

Soybeans

Autumn in the Northern Hemisphere is harvest time for soybeans. The soybean harvest has a direct impact on supply in the market. If it is a good harvest, supply will increase, which should lower the price of soybeans. If it is a poor harvest, supply will fall, which should increase the price of soybeans.

Sugar

Autumn in the Northern Hemisphere is also *harvest* time for sugarcane and sugar beets. The sugarcane and sugar beet harvest has a direct impact on supply in the market. If it is a good harvest, supply will increase, which should lower the price of sugar. If it is a poor harvest, supply will fall, which should increase the price of sugar. Spring in the Southern Hemisphere is *planting* time for sugarcane and sugar beets. The sugarcane and sugar beet planting season has a direct impact on supply in the market. If it is a productive planting season, supply will increase, which should decrease the price of sugar. If it is a poor planting season, supply will decrease, which should increase the price of sugar.

Coffee

Spring in the Southern Hemisphere is blooming time for coffee. The coffee blooming season has a direct impact on supply in the market. If it is a good blooming season, supply will increase, which should decrease the price of coffee. If it is a bad blooming season, supply will decrease, which should increase the price of coffee.

CHAPTER 6

TRADING FUTURES USING MULTIPLE TIMEFRAMES

Trading Futures Using Multiple Timeframes

Futures markets across the globe are able to function efficiently because during any given trading session, there is a steady supply of traders who want to buy futures contracts while other traders want to sell them. A trader's desire to buy or sell is influenced by their strategy, their goal and their chart timeframe. Short-term traders and long-term traders will see dramatically different things on their charts because they are scanning very different charts. Short-term traders are probably looking at 1-minute to 15-minute charts, while long-term traders are probably looking at daily, weekly or monthly charts.

Trends, support and resistance lines, and technical indicators look much different on a 5-minute chart to the way they look on a daily chart. For example you may look at a 5-minute chart of gold and see that the price appears to be in a downtrend. Yet if you switch your settings to a daily chart you may see that the price has been in an uptrend for months.

So which chart is accurate? Is gold in an uptrend or is it in a downtrend? The answer is that both charts are correct. It all depends on your perspective and your trading timeframe. If you are a shorter-term trader, you should be focusing on shorter-term charts and trends. If you are a longer-term trader, you should be focusing on longer-term charts and trends. However if you can get both the shorter-term trends and the longer-term trends to line up, you increase the odds of success in your favor.

To get a more comprehensive idea of what trending and support and resistance forces are influencing the futures contracts that you are tracking, you should analyze the following three charts (timeframes) in your technical analysis: Trend Chart(Long-term chart), Signal Chart, Timing Chart(Shorter-term chart). Once you have analyzed each timeframe, you can put them all together to confirm a good probability setup for a trade.

Trend Chart

The trend chart, as the name suggests, helps you to identify the dominant trend with which you should be looking to trade. If the price in the trend chart is trending upward, you should be looking to buy the futures contract. If the price in the trend chart is trending downward, you should be looking to sell the futures contract.

To identify the timeframe you should be using for your trend chart, you first need to identify the timeframe you ordinarily use on your signal charts. Once you have identified the timeframe of your signal chart you should include another timeframe to find the timeframe that you should be using on your trend chart.

The following is a list of common signal-chart timeframes. Use it to identify the optimal timeframe for your trend chart:

1-minute signal chart	15-minute to 30-minute trend chart
5-minute signal chart	1-hour trend chart
15-minute to 30-minute signal chart	4-hour trend chart
1-hour signal chart	1-day trend chart
1-day signal chart	1-week trend chart
1-week signal chart	1-month trend chart

For example if you typically trade futures contracts looking at a 1-hour chart, you should use a 1-day chart for your trend chart. If you typically trade futures contracts looking at a 15-minute chart, you should use a 4-hour chart for your trend chart.

Once you have identified the timeframe you should be using for your trend chart, you should determine the overall trend on the chart using support and resistance levels or moving averages.

You can see on the weekly chart for the Australian dollar that the diagonal support level indicates that this futures contract is in an uptrend.

Figure 1 - Trend Chart

If there is an uptrend on your trend chart, you should be looking for buy entry signals on your signal chart. If there is a downtrend on your trend chart, you should be looking for sell signals on your signal chart. Once you have identified the trend you need to identify profitable trading signals.

One of the many benefits you will enjoy as you use multiple timeframes in your trading is that you will see the futures market from the perspectives of many different types of traders. By looking at both short-term and long-term charts you will be more aware of what both short-term and long-term traders are paying attention to. This will help to prevent you from being caught by surprise with any sudden price movements.

Signal Chart

The signal chart is your most important chart. It provides the entry trading signals that tell you when to look for buying and selling opportunities based on the trading strategy you use. For instance if you typically use the commodity channel index (CCI) to help you identify trading signals, you will use it here on the signal chart. You don't have to use the indicator on the trend chart or the timing chart (see figure 2).

Figure 2 - Signal Chart

Using a signal chart in conjunction with a trend chart enables you to more accurately identify potentially profitable trade signals. For example if your trend chart shows the price is in an uptrend, you should only be looking for buy signals on your signal chart.

The best way to take advantage of a longer-term up-trend is to buy the futures contract. If your trend chart shows the price is in a downtrend then you should be looking for sell signals on your signal chart. The best way to take advantage of a longer-term down trend is to sell the futures contract.

In effect the trend chart allows you to ignore the less-profitable half of the trading signals you see on your signal chart. Since these trading signals are going against the longer-term trend, they will most likely be unsuccessful.

Now that you have identified your trading signals you will then need to determine exactly when to enter and exit your trades using your timing chart.

Timing Chart

The timing chart, as the name suggests, helps you to time exactly when you should enter and exit a trade. Every tick counts when you are a futures trader, so the more accurately you can identify your entry and exit points the more money you should keep in your account.

The following is a list of common signal-chart timeframes. Use it to identify the most appropriate timeframe for your timing chart:

1-minute signal chart	Tick timing chart
5-minute signal chart	1-minute timing chart
15- to 30-minute signal chart	5-minute timing chart

1-hour signal chart	15-minute timing chart
1-day signal chart	1-hour timing chart
1-week signal chart	1-day timing chart
1-month signal chart	1-week timing chart

You can use one of the following two methods when pinpointing your entry and exit signals on your timing charts:

1. You can identify the trend and support and resistance levels

2. You can use the same technical indicator you use to generate your trading signals

Identify trend and support and resistance - if you see a buy entry on your signal chart, you could expect to see the price on an uptrend on the timing chart. You also expect to see that the futures contract price is closer to support than it is to resistance. This tells you that the futures contract has room to move higher before hitting resistance. Be aware if it has just broken up through resistance, it should continue to move higher.

Using a technical indicator - if you use a technical indicator, for example, the commodity channel index (CCI) on your signal chart to generate trade signals, you can use that same indicator on your timing chart to help you identify when to enter or exit your trade.

For example if you did indeed use the CCI on your signal chart, and it gave you a buy signal, you would add the CCI to your timing chart and make sure that it was giving you a buy signal on the timing chart as well. If the CCI is not giving a buy signal on the timing chart, you should wait until it gives a buy signal on the timing chart before you enter the trade (see **Figure 3**).

Figure 3 - Timing Chart

High-Probability Trade Setup

Let us take a look at what a high-probability trade setup looks like using the multiple timeframe trading approach. We will be looking at an example of crude oil using a weekly chart as the trend chart, a daily chart as the signal chart, and a 1-hour chart as the timing chart.

First you should look at your trend chart to identify in which direction the instrument is trending. As you can see on the crude oil weekly chart, the price has been on an uptrend for some time now (see **Figure 4**). It would be unwise to fight this trend and try to sell the futures contract.

Figure 4 - Trend Chart (High-Probability Trade Setup)

Next you should look at the signal chart to identify an appropriate buy signal for crude oil. In this example we are looking at using the commodity channel index (CCI) to generate the trading signal. You can see on the daily crude oil chart that the CCI gave a buy signal on 4 May as it crossed from below -100 to above -100. The futures contract price was also on an up-trend at that same time (see **Figure 5**).

Figure 5 - Signal Chart (High-Probability Trade Setup)

Finally you should look at the timing chart to identify an appropriate time to buy crude oil. You can see on the 1-hour chart that the price is trending higher and finding support along an up-trending support level (see **Figure 6**).

Figure 6 - Timing Chart (High-Probability Trade Setup)

When you can see that the trading signal generated on the signal chart corresponds with both the trend on the trend chart and the price movement on the timing chart you should be confident that your trade has a good possibility of being profitable.

Using several timeframes provides you with more accurate trading information. Better information typically leads to better trades. Better trades lead to more profits and a happier you.

CHAPTER 7

INTERMARKET ANALYSIS

The futures market is the most diverse global financial market. While no other financial market can compare to the diversity of the futures market, other financial markets do have an impact on the futures market. For instance the U.S. bond market can influence the value of the U.S. Dollar Index futures contract just as the Japanese yen can affect the value of the Nikkei 225 Index futures contract.

To become a successful futures trader you will need to recognize the relationships that exist among the world's financial markets and comprehend how these relationships may affect the futures contracts you are trading.

Sometimes you can receive an early warning of what is going to happen in the futures market by watching what is currently happening in other financial markets. For example if you see the value of the AUD/USD currency pair rising quickly, you can look for a corresponding rise in the value of the gold futures contract. Once you know what to look out for, you can take advantage of the same correlations that the large institutional investors are watching. In this section we will be focusing on how the following markets affect the futures market: forex, bond, stock.

The Forex Market and the Futures Market

The rise of global demand for commodities has tied the futures market and the forex market closer together. Virtually every country around the world has to import some of the commodities it consumes. To buy these commodities importers typically must exchange their currency for the currency of the country from which they are importing their goods. This transaction drives the demand for the exporter's currency higher, with a corresponding increase in the value of that currency. This transaction also drives the supply of the importer's currency higher and therefore the value of that currency decreases.

Three of the major currencies - the Canadian dollar (CAD), the Australian dollar (AUD) and the New Zealand dollar (NZD) are closely related to and influenced by commodity values because they are major commodity exporters. As the price of commodities rises the value of these currencies typically rises. As the price of commodities falls the value of these currencies typically falls.

Each of these commodity currencies, as they are known amongst forex traders, is correlated with a different commodity. For example gold futures are highly correlated with the Australian dollar. As the price of the Australian dollar rises the value of gold futures typically also increase. As the price of the Australian dollar dips the value of gold futures also falls. While this correlation is not perfect it is worth paying attention to.

Futures traders can also buy and sell futures contracts that directly represent the currencies themselves. You can buy the futures contract for the Canadian dollar if you think this currency is going to increase in value. Or, you can sell the futures contract for the Japanese yen if you believe this currency is going to decrease in value. Paying attention to what is happening in the forex market during the trading sessions could therefore lead you to greater profits in your futures trading.

The Bond Market and the Futures Market

The global bond market is the second largest financial market in the world. Governments, institutions and individual investors all participate actively in the global bond market. Each one of these market participants is looking for the same thing, a profitable return on investment.

Government bonds make up the largest percentage of the global bond market. These bonds are typically viewed as risk-free investments because they are backed by the full goodwill and faith of national governments. However not all government bonds are created equal or achieve equality. Some governments pay a higher interest rate for their bonds than others. International investors take these interest rates into consideration when they are deciding where to invest their money. Typically bonds with higher interest rates are more attractive to investors, as long as the economies backing the bonds are relatively stable.

Investors who desire to buy government bonds must buy these bonds with the currency of the represented government. If international investors wish to buy U.S. government bonds then they must first exchange their currencies for U.S. dollars. This increased demand for U.S. dollars drives up the value of the U.S. Dollar Index futures contract. At the same time the increased supply of some international currencies on the market drives down the value of the futures contracts for those currencies.

Knowing which governments offer higher interest rates on their government bonds, and likewise which bonds are gaining popularity among international investors, will help you to identify which currency futures contracts to buy and which currency futures contracts to sell. Fortunately for traders the international bond market rarely changes directions instantaneously. Instead it cycles in longer-term and somewhat predictable trends that you can exploit.

You can also trade futures contracts on the government bonds themselves. If you see that demand for Japanese or Swiss bonds is increasing, for instance, you can buy the futures contract for either of these bonds

Stock Markets and the Futures Market

Individual investors around the world seem to watch stocks more closely than any other market. Stocks are exciting, they have been around for a while and most individual investors can relate to the companies in which they are buying stock. When stocks are performing well, money from around the globe flows in to buy the hot stocks. When stocks are performing poorly, money flows out as international investors sell their shares.

Futures investors can take advantage of the general increases and decreases in stock markets around the world by investing or trading in the futures contract representing the indices from the major global stock markets. For instance, to take advantage of a rising stock market in France, a futures investor can buy the futures contract for the CAC 40. Likewise, to take advantage of a falling market in the United Kingdom, a futures investor can sell the futures contract for the FTSE 100.

Globalization has also made it easier for investors from one country to invest in the stock markets of other countries. If investors see that stocks in the United Kingdom are performing well, they will look to buy those stocks. If they see that stocks in Japan are starting to outperform stocks in Europe, they may redirect their money out of the U.K. and put it into Japan in the hope of earning higher rates of return on their investments.

Stocks are priced in the local currency. To invest in stocks in the United Kingdom foreign investors must first convert their currencies into British Pounds. This increased demand for British Pounds drives up the value of British Pound futures contracts. As this occurs the increased supply of international currencies on the market, a supply that is disproportionate to demand, drives the value of the futures contracts for these currencies lower.

Futures investors watch closely how the stock markets in major countries are performing. If the stock market in one country begins outperforming the stock market in another country then futures investors know that other investors are likely to consider moving their money from the country with the weaker stock market to the country with the stronger stock market. This will drive up the value of the futures contract representing the currency of the country with the stronger stock market. And, meanwhile, the value of the futures contract representing the currency of the country with the weaker stock market will be down. By buying the futures contract for the currency from the country with the stronger stock market, and by selling the futures contract for the currency from the country with the weaker stock market, you can potentially make a handsome profit.

CHAPTER 8

SPREAD STRATEGIES

Spread Strategies

Futures traders are not limited to simply buying and selling one futures contract at a time to take advantage of price movements in the market. They have the ability to buy and sell offsetting contracts in what is known as a spread trade.

Spreads take on various forms but they all have two things in common:

1. They provide a hedge against adverse price movement

2. They are designed to take advantage of the changes in price relationships between two futures contracts.

Spreads provide a hedge against adverse price movement because you simultaneously buy and sell futures contracts when you enter a hedge. As the value of one contract goes up the value of the other contract goes down. For instance if you incur losses on the futures contract you bought as part of the spread, you can partially offset them with the gains you will realize on the contract you sold as part of the spread. Conversely if you incur losses on the futures contract you sold as part of the spread, you can partially offset them with the gains you will realize on the contract you bought as part of the spread.

Spreads take advantage of changes in price relationships. Imagine, for instance, that you see crude oil futures contracts trading on one exchange for $99 per barrel and crude oil futures trading on another exchange for $100 per barrel. You could enter a spread trade by buying the crude oil futures contract that was trading at $99 per barrel and selling the crude oil futures contract that was trading at $100 per barrel. If the two prices eventually converge, you will make a profit.

In this section we will be focusing on the following three types of spread trades: Inter-delivery spreads, Inter-commodity spreads, Inter-exchange spreads

Inter-Delivery Spreads

An inter-delivery spread is one in which a trader buys a futures contract with a certain delivery month and simultaneously sells the same futures contract with a different delivery month on the same exchange. Here's the simple breakdown:

Futures Contract:	Same
Delivery (Expiration) Month:	Different
Exchange:	Same

Inter-delivery spreads are also sometimes referred to as intra-market spreads or calendar spreads.

For example if you want to buy the July Chicago wheat contract (traded on the Chicago Board of Trade, or CBOT) because you believe prices are going to go up in the short term, but you want to hedge some of your exposure to the downside. You can accomplish this by buying the July wheat contract and simultaneously selling the September wheat contract. If the price of wheat increases in the short term, the price of the July wheat contract will probably increase faster than the price of the September wheat contract causing you to make more money on the July contract than you will lose on the September contract. However, if the price of wheat decreases in the short term, the price of the July wheat contract will also probably decrease faster than the price of the September wheat contract, causing you to lose some money on the July contract but enabling you to offset some of your losses with your gains on the September contract.

Traders divide inter-delivery spreads into two categories: bull spreads and bear spreads. A bull spread is an inter-delivery spread where you buy the nearby contract (the contract that will expire the soonest) and sell the deferred contract (the contract that will expire the latest). Traders utilize bull spreads when they believe prices are going to increase in the near-term.

The example above of buying the July wheat contract and selling September's equivalent is a good example of a bull spread.

A bear spread is an inter-delivery spread where you sell the nearby contract and buy the later month contract. Traders utilize bear spreads when they believe prices are going to decrease in the near-term.

For example, if you want to sell the July wheat contract because you believe prices are going to go down in the short term but you want to hedge some of your exposure to the upside. You can accomplish this by selling the July wheat contract and simultaneously buying the September wheat contract. If the price of wheat decreases in the short term then the price of the July wheat contract will probably decrease faster than the price of the September wheat contract causing you to make more money on the July contract than you will lose on the September contract. On the other hand if the price of wheat increases in the short term then the price of the July wheat contract will also probably increase faster than the price of the September wheat contract, causing you to lose some money on the July contract but allowing you to offset some of those losses by your gains on the September contract.

Inter-Commodity Spreads

An inter-commodity spread is a spread in which a trader buys a futures contract with a certain delivery month and simultaneously sells a different, but related, futures contract with the same delivery month on the same exchange. Here is the execution example:

Futures Contract:	Different
Delivery (Expiration) Month:	Same
Exchange:	Same

Imagine again that you want to buy the July Chicago wheat contract because you believe prices are going to go up in the short term, but you want to hedge some of your exposure to the downside. However you don't currently see any price advantage in using an inter-delivery spread. Instead you decide to use an inter-commodity spread and hedge the risk you face (as a consequence of buying a July wheat contract) by selling a July Chicago corn contract.

Wheat and corn are two different commodities but they are related. They both have relatively similar growing seasons, both are grain, and both are important in the global food supply. Now, however, you believe the price of wheat is going to increase faster than the price of corn. To take advantage of this price discrepancy you decide to buy the July wheat contract and sell the July corn contract. If the price of wheat increases faster in the short term than the price of corn, the price of the July wheat contract will probably increase faster than the price of the July corn contract allowing you to make more money on the July wheat contract than you will lose on the July corn contract. On the other hand if the price of wheat decreases faster in the short term than the price of corn, the price of the July wheat contract will also probably decrease faster than the price of the July corn contract causing you to lose some money on the July wheat contract but enabling you to offset some of your losses with your gains on the July corn contract.

Inter-Exchange Spreads

An inter-market spread is a spread in which a trader buys a futures contract with a set delivery month and simultaneously sells the same futures contract with the same delivery month on a different exchange. Here is the breakdown:

Futures Contract:	Same
Delivery (Expiration) Month:	Same
Exchange:	Different

Inter-exchange spreads are also sometimes referred to as inter-market spreads. Imagine that you want to buy the July Chicago wheat contract because you believe prices are going to rise in the short term, but that you also want to hedge some of your exposure to the downside. However, instead of hedging by using an inter-delivery spread or an inter-commodity spread, you decide to use an inter-exchange spread by hedging your long July Chicago wheat contract with a short July Kansas City wheat contract (traded on the Kansas City Board of Trade).

Chicago wheat and Kansas City wheat are quite similar. If one contract is trading at a higher price than another contract, you can buy the contract that is trading at the lower price and sell the contract that is trading at the higher price. By doing so you are buying low and selling high. If the two prices eventually converge once more then you will make a profit.

CHAPTER 9

DIVERSIFICATION

Diversification

Diversification is the practice of spreading your funds across a broad range of unrelated investments. Just like a football coach strategically places his players across the field to take advantages of changes in the game and exploit weaknesses of the opponent, you should be looking to strategically place your money across the futures market to be prepared to profit from whatever sector of the market that may begin to move.

Diversification can help protect your trading portfolio from sudden and deep losses. Let us say if you were to take all of your money and buy futures contracts on crude oil only to see the price of oil turn around and plummet in a single day. It would not take too big of a move to wipe out your entire account. Now imagine if you were to take some of your money and buy a few futures contracts on crude oil, a few futures contracts on corn, a few futures contracts on the S&P 500 and a few futures contracts on gold. Even if the price of oil dropped dramatically causing you to lose money on that trade you would still have three other trades that had not been affected by the change in the price of oil.

Obviously, you should not invest in random futures contracts just to diversify your account. You must always believe the trade you are making has the potential to be a profitable trade. But you should look to spread your risk across multiple attractive trades.

Diversification comes in different forms and sizes. In this section, we will take a look at two ways to profitably diversify your account: Commodity Diversification, Strategy Diversification.

Commodity Diversification

Perhaps the most obvious and straightforward form of diversification is diversifying amongst various commodities. As mentioned, chances are low that you will lose money on a crude oil contract, a corn contract, an S&P 500 contract and a gold contract at the same time. These futures contracts are not all affected by the same market forces. Conversely, some futures contracts are closely related. And if you only invest in closely related futures contracts, you could lose money on each contract. For instance, crude oil and natural gas are closely related, corn and wheat are closely related, the S&P 500 and the FTSE 100 are closely related and gold and silver are closely related.

Traders who achieve optimal commodity diversification look to spread their trades out among the various futures sectors. To review, the following sectors comprise the commodity futures category:

- Agriculture

- Base Metals

- Energies

- Meats

- Precious Metals

- Softs

The following sectors comprise the financial Futures category:

- Bonds

- Currencies

- Short-term Interest Rates

- Stock Indices

To put it in perspective, you have many futures sectors to choose from when you are a futures trader. You do not need to limit yourself to just one or two of those sectors. You can trade a contract in the softs sector, the bonds sector, the energies sector and the agriculture sector and diversify your risk.

Naturally, you should conduct a thorough analysis before placing any trade. Remember, you should not diversify among random contracts just for diversity's sake. You should always have a reason to buy or sell a specific contract.

If you are just getting started in your futures trading, it may take a while before you feel comfortable trading contracts from all the futures sectors, and that is just fine. There is no pressure to trade everything and specializing is often best in the beginning.

Strategy Diversification

Diversification relates not only to *which* futures contracts you choose to buy and sell but also to *how* you decide to buy or sell those contracts. Strategy diversification can be just as important to your overall success as a futures trader as commodity diversification.

You have learned many different trading strategies throughout this book. You have learned about trading with price patterns, trading with technical indicators, and trading various spread strategies. Now it's time to begin using these various strategies.

For example, if you are looking across the different market sectors because you want to maintain a healthy amount of commodity diversification, and you notice that the futures contracts in one of the sectors (ex. precious metals) are moving sideways while the futures contracts in one of the other market sectors (ex. energies) are moving higher in a strong up trend. Certainly, you could diversify your account and buy some contracts in the precious metals sectors and some contracts in the energies sector and achieve a high level of commodity diversification, but is that really the most effective way to deploy your money into these trades?

Buying the contracts in the energies sector is probably a good idea because those contracts are currently in up trends. However, buying the contracts in the precious metals sectors seems like a waste of time because those contracts are channeling sideways. Perhaps a more effective use of your money would be to implement a spread strategy, like an inter-delivery spread, that takes advantage of futures contracts that are moving sideways. By doing so, you would not only ensure that you achieve your desired level of commodity diversification but also ensure that you are using the appropriate trading strategy for what the market provides you. Try taking aspects of this approach with your futures trading. If you find one strategy is not working, try another one. You are only limited by your imagination and your willingness to be creative.

In the end, if you can diversify your trading across multiple futures contracts and implement a few different trading strategies to take advantage of whatever circumstances the market is throwing at you, you will find you are well on your way to becoming a successful futures trader.

CHAPTER 10

EXCHANGE TRADED FUNDS

Exchange traded funds (ETFs) are investment funds that are traded on stock exchanges. While they are not mutual funds, they do offer all of the benefits of diversification that you would enjoy when trading a mutual fund. ETFs also enjoy all of the benefits of liquidity that you have from trading individual shares. In plain terms ETFs are funds that trade like a stock.

ETFs offer instant diversification because, when you buy an ETF, you buy a piece of a fund that incorporates multiple assets. ETFs are like a large asset pool into which fund managers place various assets such as shares, bonds and commodities. When you buy an ETF you buy wholesale ownership of the pool and its contents as a whole, not piecemeal ownership of the individual contents.

You can make money with an ETF. As the value of the assets within the pool increases so does the overall value of the pool. Conversely, as the value of the assets within the pool decreases so does the overall value of the pool. In other words as the assets within an ETF increase in value the value of the ETF increases, and as the assets within an ETF decrease in value the value of the ETF decreases.

Instant Diversification

ETFs give you the ability to simultaneously own multiple assets without having to buy each asset individually. Imagine, for instance, the trading costs that would accumulate and the capital you would need to have in your account if you had to buy each share within the S&P 500 individually.

Diversification can also help protect you from unsystematic risk. For instance if you own only one of the shares in the Nikkei 225 Index, and that share loses value, you will lose money on your investment. However if you own the entire Nikkei 225 Index via an ETF, and that same share goes down, you have 224 other shares around it that are likely to ensure the value of the entire index either remains stable or climbs higher.

Many of the most popular ETFs track broad market indices. The following are just a few examples:

S&P 500

Dow Jones Industrial Average

FTSE 100

DAX Index

Nikkei 225

FTSE/Xinhua China 25 Index

NASDAQ 100

CAC 40 Index

Many ETFs also track various market sectors such as the following:

Information technology

Energy

Materials

Industrials

Telecommunication

Utilities

Health care

Financials

Open Market Trading

ETFs are freely traded on stock exchanges just like regular shares. As long as the stock exchanges on which the ETFs trade are open you can buy or sell any ETF. This is an advantage over mutual funds.

Mutual funds typically are only traded at the end of the market day once all of the assets within the funds can be valued. At that point the funds are assigned a closing value for the day, and you can buy or sell the funds at the closing value. Unfortunately during trading days when the assets within the funds are losing value you must hold onto the funds until the end of the day regardless of how much value the funds are losing. To conclude, whether you see the value of an ETF increasing or decreasing during the trading day you can buy or sell the ETF to take advantage of the price movement.

You can protect your ETF trades by setting stop loss orders. Because ETFs are freely traded you can set stop-loss orders that may take you out of your trades during the market day when your pre-determined price is hit. If you were trading mutual funds to obtain diversification, you would not have this ability because you can only buy or sell mutual funds at the end of the trading day after the markets have closed. So it wouldn't matter if your trigger price was hit during the market day because you would not be able to exit your trade.

Stop Loss Orders

Stop loss orders allow you to implement appropriate risk management measures in your account. Consequently, you can simultaneously protect your investment capital by both diversification and stop-loss orders.

Lower Fees

When you give your money to a manager to invest you usually have to pay that manager a fee. Typically the more active a role the manager plays in the investment decisions the larger the fee you will have to pay. ETFs usually have lower fees because they are passively managed, unlike many funds, including mutual funds that are actively managed.

Many ETFs track a specific index, market sector and so on. Since the composition of most stock indexes and share sectors barely changes, the managers of most ETFs do not often need to change the holdings within the fund. Consequently, because these managers do not play as active a role they charge a lower fee.

Most mutual fund managers, on the other hand, make daily decisions regarding what assets they are going to add to their portfolios, what assets they are going to keep in their portfolios and what assets they are going to remove from their portfolios. This active management and the trading fees it produces boost the fees that mutual fund managers charge their clients.

CONCLUSION

Thank you for making it through to the end of *Futures Trading Strategies.* Let's hope it was informative and able to provide you with the first set of tools that you need to achieve your goals of trading using futures and making money with them.

The next step is to test your skills at trading and build up your risk capital so that you can make additional trades. This will give you the motivation that you need to succeed.

I have several other books on different aspects of trading and asset classes please check them out!

PROFILE OF THE AUTHOR

Wayne Walker is the director of a global capital markets education and consulting firm (gcmsonline.info). He has several years experience in leading and coaching teams of Investment Advisors and has managed top performing teams in the Private Client Group based on Bench Mark Earnings (BME).

www.ingramcontent.com/pod-product-compliance
Lightning Source LLC
Chambersburg PA
CBHW071725170526
45165CB00005B/2158